Elizabeth's Story

Vera Klaassen DeMay

ISBN-13:978-1495970634
ISBN-10: 1495970639

ACKNOWLEDGEMENTS

I WOULD LIKE TO THANK THE PEOPLE WHO HAVE MADE THIS BOOK POSSIBLE BY ENCOURAGING ME TO KEEP GOING: RAE ANN NORELL, PAM MALONEY , JANE FREUND, PETER LEAVELL, ANN KELLER, SHERRILL NIELSEN, AND WITHOUT THE SUPPORT OF MY SISTERS: SHIRLEY LEE AND LINDA HORTON, THIS BOOK WOULD NOT HAVE GOTTEN INTO PRINT.

DEDICATION

This book is dedicated to descendants of Elizabeth Toews Klaassen.

My sisters, Linda Horton and Shirley Lee

My children: Jeanice McCall and Joseph DeMay

My grandchildren: Adrienne McCall, Ashleigh McCall, and Christopher McCall, Jr.

My Nieces and nephews: Faithann Basore, John Horton, Joy Montoya, Levi Horton, Amy Pickering, Jason, Eric, Carla, and Bryan Lee

My great-nieces and nephews: Kimera, Josh, Caleb, and Sarah Basore, Emry Dillard, Mandolin, Samantha, and Maria Montoya, Luke Pickering.

CONTENTS

PART III

Elizabeth Klaassen

Preface

I am the oldest daughter of Elizabeth Toews. My mother's origins and early years have always been a great mystery to me. She never talked much about her journey from Russia to Canada in 1924, when she was six years old. When asked, she would say, "Oh we traveled by train to the Baltic Sea and then by ship to Canada." It wasn't until a family reunion in 2008 that I learned about that journey through the documentary called *And When They Shall Ask: The Migration of the Russian Mennonites out of Russia*. Her parents and four children made it out along with about 1,000 people sponsored by the Canadian Mennonite Committee on Colonization.

Mother was born in 1918 and passed away in 2008. She lived ninety years, seven months and three days. Her life's journey took her from the village of Tiegenhagen in South Russia, to Winnipeg, Manitoba in Canada, to southern California, and finally to Kent, Washington. She gave birth to three girls – two born in Canada and one in California.

I feel compelled to tell her story for the benefit of her children, grand-children, great-grand-children, and future generations of descendants of the Toews family. I hope to give understanding to her descendants, the many who do not even know about this incredible woman and her struggles and challenges. I tell her story in her voice based on stories shared, my research, and my imagination.

January 14, 2013
Vera Klassen DeMay

Vera Klaassen DeMay

Prologue
Village Life in Tiegenhagen

Beautiful acacia and oak trees lined the streets of our picturesque little village and low, white-washed houses surrounded the large meeting house located in its center. People greeted one another with a hearty, *"Goan Dach!"* (Good day) when they met on the street. Everyone knew their neighbors whose joys and sorrows alike were shared with one another. Life continued in peace and calm.

April brought mild spring breezes. The tender violets at the edge of the pasture along with the tulips and crocuses in the gardens began blossoming after being dormant during the long winter. Everything kindled with new hope, as evidenced by the budding trees and shrubs and the cheerful chirping of the birds in the forest. The children sang a well-known spring song:

> *Gentle breezes I feel, Golden spring is coming*
> *my longing is for the distance, Hand me my walking staff.*
> *Where the white mists are rising, around the*
> *circle of blue mountains,*
> *there I will walk, hand me my walking staff.*[i]

It was a village custom to bring the cattle home from the pasture for the night. Every cow knew its home. The village children stood on the side of the street with grandfather, surrounded by dust clouds, and observed the events with great interest. He even made a little whip for us to pretend we were herding the cows too.

Mothers didn't like their children watching this evening spectacle because they were always worried something might happen to them.

The hard work in the fields during summer harvest time was followed by cozy winter evenings. Our family sat near the warm tiled stove, comforted by the glow of a coal-oil lamp. Papa told stories while Mother sat in front of her whirring spinning wheel, making socks which she sold at the village market place.

The winds of autumn swept over the empty stubble fields and the golden wheat was safely in storage. Heavy laden fruit trees were harvested, and baskets filled with apples and pears were stored in the cellars. The red watermelons and yellow melons were safely stored in the hay shed. Now we could look forward with confidence to winter.

After the harvest, just before the cold winter set in, the Big Day for butchering arrived. Everyone in the village helped. Lard boiled in large vats, and the women made sausages and pork rind while the smoking sheds filled up with large hams and sausages. After a hard day's labor, the crowning touch was a special meal, and everyone participated in the feast. Such were the days I was born into in 1918.

Soon however, dark clouds were on the political horizon. No one had any idea what they would bring. My parents and our villagers remained blissfully unaware of the storms which would scatter our people into the four corners of the world. Perhaps it was a good thing we did not know what was to come.

Practically overnight the greatest disaster erupted over the Mennonites in Russia. Within a short time, everything our ancestors had built during an entire century was completely destroyed. We were soon to experience that happiness here on earth is as fragile as glass.[ii]

PART I

My name is Elizabeth Toews, I was born February 23, 1918 in the village of Tiegenhagen, in the Molotschna district of the Ukraine. This is my story.

Vera Klaassen DeMay

Chapter 1

Days of Terror

I come from a close-knit community of German speaking Dutch Mennonites that settled the Molotschna region of the Ukraine, Russia in pursuit of religious freedoms in the early 19th Century. My people had lived there in peace and prosperity, enjoying the many benefits and freedoms granted to them by Empress Catherine II. The Empress granted them religious and educational freedoms, and recognized their pacifist way of life and exempted them from military service.

These special privileges enjoyed by the Mennonites contributed to the Russian peoples jealously of them, and led to mounting pressure on the Russian Government to take those freedoms away. Around 1871 the Mennonites started losing those freedoms and the Military service exemption was taken away. Conscription was instituted for all, though eventually the Russian government allowed for alternative service such as forestry and industrial work or noncombatant medical service during times of war. Like my father who served as a medic with the Russian Army during World War I.

Toward the end of the war the German Army was retreating from the Russian Army. They left firearms and other equipment behind. In time, the Russian government, thinking they knew the exact number of rifles left in each village, issued orders to each village to hand over that number of rifles.

In 1919, three months after the war had ended, the ruthless partisan army of Nestor Ivanovich Makhno invaded the Molotschna. Makhno, son of a Russian peasant born in the village of Gulyaypole, about forty miles northeast of the Molotschna, had developed a vengeful hatred for the Mennonite colonies. His "baptism by fire" was well known and feared in the region.[iii]

Uncle Peter taken prisoner

One day, the gangs came to our peaceful village of Tiegenhagen and other outlying communities. Soldiers on horseback entered and demanded to see the mayor. Two men were taken hostage from Tiegenhagen. One was Uncle Peter Kornelsen. He was permitted to take a pillow and a blanket with him and to say goodbye to his family. Up until now, we had hardly been aware of the war because we lived in the safety and security. We had no idea of the far-reaching effects of these political events. Uncle Peter was taken to Halbstadt under heavy guard along with many others. Five other prisoners were already under heavy guard in Reverend G. Harder's basement.

All of them, including the Harders, were taken to the backyard and shot in the back. This terrible news spread quickly through our communities. Everyone worried about Uncle Peter, who was the minister at the Mennonite Brethren Church.

Tanta Maria was sick with worry that her husband would be the next victim. Somewhere deep inside her she found the courage and determination to go to Halbstdt to be near him. Many women would not have been able to find such courage. After finding suitable accommodations, she made her way to the town administrator, Mr. Bogon, who was well known for his unfriendly attitude toward the Germans. That however, did not deter Tanta Maria. Tear fully, she pleaded for the release of her husband. Mr. Bogon became angry and told her in coarse language to get out of the office.

In the meantime Uncle Peter was waiting for what was to happen next. Around two o'clock at in the morning a soldier knocked on the door and called out a name. As if struck by lightning, Uncle Peter jumped up when he heard his name called out. He was told to gather up his belongings and follow the soldier. Three other men were already on the wagon. They were all certain they were going to be taken somewhere and shot.

When the wagon crossed the bridge into Prischib, great fear arose in them. Near Prischib they came to the sand pits where many innocent people and been shot and buried there in secret. However, the wagon continued on and stopped in front of the police building. The men were ordered to get off the wagon. They were led into a dark damp cellar with no window. Fear was replaced by sheer terror. If they were not shot and killed, they would surely die in this dap, ice-cold basement.

Days and weeks of uncertainty followed for the villagers. It was a great comfort to Tanta Maria to have all of her sisters nearby. She was especially close to my mother. The whole community around Tiegenhagen prayed without ceasing for their leader. Neighbors also helped in any way they could. In times of trouble and misery, boundaries of church membership disappear. One feels the pain and distress of their brothers, their neighbors, regardless in which congregation one is listed as a member.

We found comfort in the psalms during these stressful times. Psalm 32:7 was one of them.

*"Thou are my hiding place; thou shalt
preserve me from trouble; thou shalt compass me about with
songs of deliverance. Selah. I will instruct thee and teach thee in
the way thou shalt go."*

One night the prisoners received word of their death sentence. They were to be shot. After all the previous fears and threats, this news came almost as a relief. This terrible uncertainty would finally be over. The question that weighed heavily on each one was, how would their families get the word? Posters were posted in the villages announcing the execution of the prisoners. Uncle Peter's name was on that list.

Relatives, friends and neighbors soon gathered at Tante Marie's home to give comfort. Expecting to find her very distraught, she was quite composed. Tante Marie was not convinced that her husband would die

.

A fur coat for freedom

Somehow one of the policemen had discovered that Uncle Peter and Mr Schmidt had fur coats at home. They began a scheme in which they would steal the papers accusing the prisoners and request as payment in exchange, the fur coats.

One night a knock on the door woke a startled Tante Marie. The soldier at the door immediately spoke in an reassuring voice that he was there with news from her husband and handed her the note. Tante Marie looked at it and confirmed that it was her husband's handwriting. In it, Uncle Peter stated that he was still alive and the she was to give the soldier his fur coat. That would ease his situation a lot. Without hesitation the soldier got the fur coat. After a hardy meal, the soldier asked if she would like to see her husband once more. Tante Marie grabbed her hat and coat and followed. What joy erupted, they only had a few minutes together and such a meeting was extremely risky for all of them.

The decision regarding the prisoners came a few days later. The soldier delivering the message stood at the door, silent. The tensions were mounting. Finally Uncle Peter could contain himself no longer and asked excitedly: "Comrade, what did the court decide?"

"They decided not to shoot you. The population of Halbstadt is against more shedding of blood." He replied.

They were released that night but not before hearing from Comrade Bogon . He had a farewell address to give.

"You Mennonites! You call yourself non-resistant and what did we find among you? An entire wagon load of rifles. You have blood on your hands. But you are to know one thing, the Soviet government punishes but it also forgives. Now go home and become obedient citizens of the empire!"

The decision had not reached our village so no one knew the outcome. Suddenly, in the middle of the night, a knock on the door, it was Uncle Peter, he was free.

Like a bird which is released from his narrow cage, taking flight and soaring into the air, this is how the men felt.

With the end of the war, everyone was full of hope, now good times would come again. The children continued to play in the streets, but soon more would be required of us.[iv]

Vera Klaassen DeMay

Chapter 2
The Famine of 1922

In 1922 the terrible famine came. The war-torn land had been sucked dry. Prospects for any sort of economic recovery in most of the region was very dismal by 1921. The heat and drought in the spring of 1921, the lack of draft horses and seed grain excluded any sizable planting. Every village, every farm, every household now had no food.

The attics and barns were empty. The cattle grazing in the fields were unable to provide the smallest amount of milk, then our only cow was taken by raiding bandits. Father would pass when offered food by mother and soon his belly swelled up like many others in our village. Tanta Maria and Uncle Peter somehow managed to keep a garden growing and that kept many of us alive.

Then, when things couldn't get worse, the relief we had hoped for came. The German-Russians call for help reached America. The American Relief Agency was founded and an active pioneer effort was organized to provide the much needed food. A large community kitchen was established in our village and the people began to work. Huge sheets of white buns were baked, and large vats of cocoa was made with milk and sugar. The first to receive food were the children, expectant mothers, the old and the sick, but the need was so great in general that everyone received rations.

How delicious that large bun and cocoa were. The food strengthened us. Children began to play in the streets and the adults were friendly again. We began to be hopeful for the future.

Unfortunately, help came too late for some. The statistics show that about 823 families were starving and that almost half of them died. Everyone suffered. The dear little ones in the school lost their zest for life, and their eyes lost their sparkle over time. Were it not for the active intervention of American friends, the Mennonite people would have succumbed to total annihilation at the claws of famine.[v]

Chapter 3
The Decision to Leave

"Mutti, Mutti!"[vi] I screamed, "The bad people are coming, I hear them coming! What is all the noise about? I'm scared!" My three-year-old sister Margaret and I huddled in the back corner under the small wood framed bed we shared, clutching each other in fear. I was five. It seemed like we stayed there forever waiting--- waiting for the bad people to leave. We heard screams, gun shots, horses snorting, and shouting. And, then there was silence--- dead silence.

It was dark when we finally summoned the courage to come out from our hiding place. Mutti told us to be very quiet. We were hungry and she gave us a small piece of bread which we ate quickly. We didn't dare turn on a light or light a candle and there was no fire in the wood burning stove, so we crawled into bed under several layers of quilts. We covered our heads, and soon we were warm and toasty. Our eyes fluttered to stay open. We heard Papa and Mutti whispering but couldn't understand what they were saying. It sounded very scary to us.

Daylight broke the next morning. The sun was shining, the air was crisp, and people began coming out of their homes. Our neighbor said in a loud voice, "Did you hear, they took Br Enns away last night. Br Freisen's cow was taken, and the community gathering place burned down."

"We must do something," another neighbor announced.

"But what can we do? We have a right to arm ourselves to defend our families against evil," Frau Klaassen spoke up.

Someone else disagreed saying, "But God's word says we are to turn the other cheek."

I understood nothing they were talking about. Until now, my life had been carefree and full of fun, playing with my many cousins, going to Sunday school and learning the songs. I loved our village. Food was plentiful, and the love of family helped us feel safe and secure.

Tanta Nata had the largest front porch, so my mother and aunties often gathered there to crochet. They carefully crafted items of clothing and decorative linens. This was, of course, after the chores were finished and food was prepared for the evening meal. They often broke into song, their voices blending in harmony. Now, they talked in low voices, almost whispering.

The children played in the yard, some swinging on the double swing hanging from the large oak tree that Papa had put up. The tree gave wonderful protection from the sun and was also great for climbing. "Some day when I am bigger," I thought to myself, "I will climb to the very highest point. Oh, the things I would see from there." I wondered if I would ever see what was beyond the river.

Soon, Cousin Mary Kornelsen showed up. Being the oldest cousin, she took charge and bossed us younger ones around. "Children, children, come quickly. It's time for your lesson. Sit down, boys on this side and girls on the other, very orderly. Lize, where is your brother Jake?" Mary asked.

"He left with Papa this morning early" I replied.

We sat straight up in our chairs and quietly listened while Cousin Mary told us the story from the Bible about Moses when he was a baby. His mother hid him in the reeds in the river to save him from the bad people who were killing all the baby boys. Later

Moses became the leader of his people and helped them escape from slavery in Egypt. She told us the people grumbled and complained when things didn't go their way, and that God spoke to Moses in a burning bush.

I didn't understand much of it, but it was a nice story. Cousin Mary used some hand puppets she had made to help tell the story.

Then she announced, "Girls, it's time for supper. Come in and clean up so you can help set the table. Come quick ---before the food gets cold."

Sister Agatha, my oldest sister, was already in the kitchen. Her job was to help mother with the food preparations. At ten years old she was expected to do much of the household chores. Before we could start eating, Mutti said, "Now we must thank the Lord for this food." We folded our hands, closed our eyes, and prayed in unison:

"Kom Heir Jesus, Si gast unt...[vii]

After filling our stomachs, we quickly cleaned up. It was important to get everything put away before dark because we couldn't turn on any lights. The little ones carried what they could to the sink while Agatha and Mutti put the food away. They set aside plates for Papa and Brother Jake.

It must have been way after midnight when Papa and Jake came home. They had been at a meeting with the men and Uncle Peter at the church. Something was happening. I could feel the tension in my stomach. There was talk about leaving our homeland and going to a country far away. I heard Papa say, "We will wait. Maybe the situation will improve."

Mother Agatha Toews with Brother Jake and Sister Agatha, 1915

Backside of photo

Chapter 4
Journey to Freedom

Many meetings were taking place between our community representatives, and officials from the government. The Canadian Mennonite Committee for Colonization got involved also. Lists were prepared of those wanting to emigrate. Then, something would happen, the lists would disappear and negotiations would start all over. Finally, the order came that those who wanted to leave, could. The Canadian Pacific Railroad agreed to transport the emigrants to their destinations once they arrived in Canada, however, they would need to be reimbursed. Sponsors were found. My father filled out the necessary document

One day Papa came home and announced, "Mama, it's time for us to leave. I have the papers for us to go to Canada. We can take only what we can bring in our suitcases. Please pack carefully because we will not return. We need to be ready to leave at the end of the week. Tell no one outside the family that we are leaving."

Application for Emigration with the Canadian Mennonite
Board of Colonization (side 1)[viii]

Application for Emigration with the Canadian Mennonite
Board of Colonization (side 2)[ix]

And so, on July 13, 1924, one-thousand emigrants gathered at the train station in Lichtenau, anticipating the pain of parting. The farewell was heart-rending. Family ties were broken. Some said good-bye, never to return, others said good-by, never to leave. Someone started singing: "God be with you till we meet again," and soon everyone, young and old, joined in while tears blurred their vision.

The following poem recited at the farewell event the previous day, portrays the emotional scene at the Lichtenau Station:

The train is ready for departure;
People are coming from near and far,
Walking, with spring-and ladder wagons.
Even the infant is carried there;
The air filled with dust...heaven grey;
At the Lichtenau station.

The wind blows and whistles and sings,
The child in the arms of his mother cries.
People are putting up the "Samowar"
Because one has to eat...that is for sure
Because all of them have this feeling of faintness
At the Lichtenau station.

The crowd is moving back and forth
And the hearts are heavy.
Here they are singing a song of farewell,
They know that they will never see each other again.
The man looks soberly...the woman weeps
At the Lichtenau station

Then people hurry over to the church,
They are only staying there for a brief time,
They pray and weep
And all are united in prayer.
For everyone thinks: "only trust in God!"
Whether in Canada...or Lichtenau.

The iron horse whistles and people are cold,
They lose their composure...
There is sighing and weeping – hands are shaken;
Farewell...farewell in the foreign land!"
Once more they look upon their homeland
At the Lichtenau station.

The bell rings for the last time...
One pulls up the ladder, the narrow one;
Closes the doors:
"Hand me little Lori one more time!"
And even men, grey-haired ones...
Are weeping today in Lichtenau.

The bell rings for the last time;
A sudden jerking...the train is moving! The crowd sings:
Many persons are staying behind...alone
One waves...sees nothing because of falling tears!
Forsaken lies the village of Lichtenau.[x]

It is seven o'clock in the evening, as the long freight train pulled its cargo out of the station. Those remaining are waving with tears in their eyes. Farther and farther the homeland recedes as the train travels through the steppes of Russia, past fields and pastures. The boxcars are overcrowded but no one is complaining. freedom beckons.

The full impact of what was happening didn't affect the children as much. Soon we found a little corner of the box car, and played games, sang songs, and generally were happy.

We never realized the danger we were in until, after eleven days of travelling, as we approached the border, all of a sudden the train came to a stop. There was a lot of shouting! Russian soldiers searched every car, checking everyone's documents. Finding a "discrepancy" on one, they grabbed the man and threw him off the train. We heard a gunshot. Women and children began to cry, while the men tried unsuccessfully to quiet everyone. From the corner of the boxcar we heard a small voice singing, and one by one, we all joined in.

The train began to move slowly toward the gate. "Please dear Father in Heaven," we prayed, "keep the gate open and let us pass through safely." Many were holding their breath as the train made its ponderous way through the gate. It seemed like an eternity, but at last we were free. We made it, we were in Latvia. Oh, the joy that erupted when the last car passed through to freedom.

We continued on and on. At long last, on July 24th, we boarded a small steamship, the *Marglen* on our way to South Hampton, England. We were a people without a homeland. We carried everything we owned in the world up the gangway.

The second of August, we boarded *The Empress of France* which would take us across the great Atlantic Ocean. The ocean was silvery grey in appearance, foamy waves reflected the sun. Untiringly and unceasingly the waves broke on the white-sanded shore. Gulls circled the ship hoping for a crumb. The ship moved gently in the waves, waiting to carry the homeless emigrants to a far, unknown country. We seemed to be like the waves of the sea, constantly in motion, carried into an uncertain future.

The journey across the ocean was nothing but fun for us kids. We played games, running up and down the decks. Knowing how grueling our journey had been, our elders didn't have the heart to scold us after such a fearful and exhausting journey. Approaching our new homeland on August 7th at 5:30a.m. in the morning, we saw the coast of Nova Scotia and to the right, Canada. The next day we arrived in Quebec. Europe was behind us like a bad dream. We were in a land of freedom and order.

Once aboard a Canadian Pacific Railroad train, we experienced our first introduction to this new country: bologna. It was here that many were sent different directions depending on the arrangements made by their sponsors. Once again we had to say good-bye, this time to the Kornelsen family. It was a very difficult parting, Mother and Tanta Marie wept deeply. Would the sisters ever be together again, they wondered?

xi

Last farewells at the Lichtenau Terminal on July 13, 1924

Emigrants embarking at Lichtenau, Molotschna,on July 13, 1924

PART II

Vera Klaassen DeMay

Chapter 5
Strangers in a New Land

Upon our arrival in Winnipeg, we were greeted warmly by our fellow Mennonite brethren. We were assigned to a family who took us in and helped us settle into the community. Adjustments had to be made by the newly arrived emigrants and their host families. Each regarded the other with reservation and in some cases, contempt.

In this new land we found comfort that many of our relatives from the old country were there as well. We were happy our O–ma, who was a widow, and her son Peter lived with us.

Life was hard. Papa secured a job shoveling coal for the residential homes. It was physically demanding, but he never complained. Mama had another baby the next year in November, a girl. They named her Mary or Marichen.

My siblings and I soon started school. For the most part it was very confusing. The lessons were in English. We didn't understand the language and no one took the time to teach us. Perhaps had we not stayed within our own German speaking community, we might have assimilated to our new environment, and learned to speak English more quickly.

Other factors contributed to the fact that so many did not even get through high school. When my oldest sister Agatha entered the sixth grade, she soon dropped out of school to become a domestic helper in the Jewish community. My brother Jake finished the eleventh grade and went to one year of "normal school" so he could become a teacher. However, he had bad eye sight and with no encouragement or help from home, he too dropped out. My sister Margaret continued her schooling through the tenth grade.

I made it to the seventh grade and then took odd jobs here and there, mostly house cleaning. I remember wanting to take up sewing, but Mama said it would be too hard for me and so I didn't pursue it any further. Our youngest sister Mary, entered Nursing School, but when challenged with the pressures of her studies, was not encouraged to return. There were many things we wanted to do but Mama always fearful of new experiences, found a way to keep us from our ambitions.

As the decades moved forward, World War II started in Europe. The Germans were the enemy and while we spoke the German language, we made it known we were of Dutch descent. We all lived together in one house as was the custom in those days. My brother worked for the railroad, Margaret and Mary worked in retail and my oldest sister and I worked as domestic help. Life was full of church activities, visiting our vast number of cousins, and fun times at the park. Many summers were also spent at a relative's farm.

One of our favorite past-times was the weekly Bible study with our girls-only Cousin's Club. We had frequent luncheons hosted by one of us, and we even went to a photography studio for a professional photo. I especially enjoyed singing in our church choir. I took voice lessons for a while and people said I had a good voice. I proudly practiced my scales "ah ah ah ah, hee hee hee hee."

Despite the activities we enjoyed, things were tense at home. My oldest sister was often at odds with the rest of the family and there were many arguments. Life continued to take its toll on my father. He tried to keep peace as best he could, and took over the cooking when Mama spent days in bed, often distressed over the issue of my sister Mary. After working in retail for twenty years, Mary was diagnosed with a mental illness and could no longer work. When she was on her medication, all was well. When she was not, she could get very volatile.

When World War II ended, my sisters and I were in our twenties, and there were few eligible bachelors. Many of the men returning from the War brought home wives from Europe. One by one my cousins began to marry and have children, but not my sisters and me. We wondered, "what was wrong with us?" The explanation that there were few available men didn't seem to fit which made us feel that we were getting past the marrying age. We thought one of the worst things in life was to be considered a spinster.

Back Row: Agatha, Jake, Elizabeth, Margaret
Front row: Mary, Agatha, Jacob

Young Elizabeth

Elizabeth at the lake

Elizabeth with sisters Mary and Margaret

Chapter 6
Elizabeth Meets Edmund

It was December 1947. Our community of Mennonite churches had a sing-off rally, and choirs from all over came to perform. There was one small choir from Morden that caught my attention. In back, almost hidden behind the taller girls in the front, was a very handsome dark-haired man with the most incredible bass voice.

"Who is that man?" I asked. No one seemed to know. From the list of choirs in the program I found out he was a country farmer from the Mennonite Conference. This handsome stranger kept catching my eye and then he broke into a smile that brightened up his entire face. How could I meet him?

To my delight, we ran into each other in the basement cafeteria. Approaching my table carrying a tray laden with food, he asked in his deep bass voice, "May I sit down?" I blushed and nodded consent.

He said, "My name is Edmund Klaassen".

My heart pounded as I murmured, "Happy to meet you. I'm Elizabeth."

Winter shortened our courtship so we didn't get to see each other very often. Somehow Edmund managed to make the 100 mile trip to Winnipeg to visit. When weather permitted, we took long walks and soon began talking about marriage. So when Edmund asked the question I had been longing to hear, "Will you marry me?"

My response was, "Yes, with God's help, I will marry you."

Edmund and I married on April 10, 1948, also my parents' anniversary. The church was packed with family and friends. The pipe organ played the wedding march as I walked down the aisle with my father. Edmund was waiting at the front of the sanctuary. The minister spoke the words that joined us together as husband and wife in a covenant relationship with God. It was a wonderful day.

The day after we married, my new husband took me to his farm home in the country. We would be living with Edmund's brother and wife, and their two young boys. I tried to carve out a small area to call our own but the rooms were small and the boys were always under foot. There were many chores to be completed daily: gathering eggs for breakfast, milking the cow, and keeping the house clean. I was overwhelmed.

Edmund and his brother were in the fields from before dawn until after sun set. By the time he came home after a full day's work, the meal I had prepared for him was cold. Exhausted, he crawled into bed, only to start the routine all over again in a few hours.

Elizabeth and Edmund

Vera Klaassen DeMay

Elizabeth marries Edmund Klaassen, April 10, 1948

Chapter 7
Motherhood

"I'm going crazy here, what is wrong with me?" I told my husband's 12 year old niece. "I'm crying all the time and I feel sick to my stomach. The smell of food makes me nauseated." It didn't take me long to figure out I was with child.

"Another mouth to feed in this house," was my brother-in-law's response.

I ran into our room crying. My husband, not knowing what to do, finally agreed that we would move back to Winnipeg and live with my family until we got on our feet.

On December 30, 1948, I delivered our firstborn, a daughter. We named her Elvira Irene. My family was in awe of her. My sisters, Margaret and Mary, were especially helpful. I spent a lot of time at my parents' house and walked home in time to feed my husband. What a screamer Elvira was. We were exhausted from tending to her all night. Nothing we did satisfied her.

When Edmund lost his job because of lack of sleep, we took Elvira to a doctor. By then she was nine months old. When the doctor found out I was feeding her diluted evaporated milk, he said I was basically starving her. I felt devastated about this. Once adequately fed, our baby was satisfied, slept well, and was a joy in our lives. At a year old, she pointed at our Christmas tree, and uttered her first word, *"baum."*[xiii]

Our family expanded with another daughter, Linda Elizabeth, born September 15, 1951. Linda was a very calm, content baby, with beautiful olive skin, big brown eyes, and a head full of dark hair.

With one child almost three years old and a new baby, I was filled with the challenges of taking care of my family. Still, I spent many hours at my parents' home. Elvira adored her grandfather, O-pa.

Life seemed complete. I had my husband, my daughters, and my family. And then everything changed. My husband wanted us to move to the United States, southern California to be exact. What was he thinking? Why so far away? He told me he couldn't stand working in Manitoba's sub-zero temperatures. I think the real reason was he felt my family was too interfering and had too much influence on me.

Elizabeth with Edmund and first-born daughter

Elizabeth's parents with first granddaughter

Elizabeth with baby Linda

PART III

Chapter 8
Another Homeland

It was mid-November 1952. Our bags packed, we stood on the train platform waiting for the final boarding call. My parents, sisters and brother were all in tears. My dad folded his arms around Elvira and held on for the longest time. Tenderly he laid his hand on sleeping baby Linda. He knew what this good-bye meant. Would he ever see his precious granddaughters again? One by one each of them gave their final hugs and kisses. The train porter blew the whistle. It was time to go and we stepped onto the train. My family stood on the platform in the freezing cold until the last car pulled away.

The train was crowded but we soon found two seats facing each other and settled in for the long journey, leaving Canada and entering the United States of America. The trip took three days and three nights. We pulled into our final destination, Chino, California, early in the morning. The sun was already shining, we took our coats off because we were too warm. Edmund's Uncle Bill Dalke met us at the depot. Oh the sights we saw, grove after grove of orange trees, their fruit just waiting to be picked. Was it really November? People walking the sidewalks in short-sleeved shirts, some even wearing short pants.

Uncle Bill said we could stay with him and his wife for just a few days but we would need to find a place to live as soon as possible. He could show us a few places he had already checked out. "How much money do you have, Edmund?" he asked. My husband lowered his head as he pulled out a Twenty dollar Canadian bill.

"That's it? That's all you have? What were you thinking? Bringing your family all this way with no money, no job." I took Linda to a bedroom to change her diaper as a loud one-way conversation ensued, my husband saying nothing.

"He gave us three-hundred dollars as a loan to get started but he expected to be paid back within a month." Edmund whispered to me when he found me. "He is taking me to look at a house in Ontario."

"I will start packing our belongings while you're gone," I replied.

We moved into that house in Ontario two days later. With the remaining $225, we bought a car for $50 and had money left over for food. A month later we had to move again as we didn't have any money and no job. Some people at our new Mennonite church helped us out with food and one of the men told Edmund about a job he should look into. We were barely settled in when to my surprise my mother-in-law came to visit. Uncle Bill was her brother. She stayed and stayed what seemed like forever. She was a severe woman and I felt her displeasure of me constantly.

Elizabeth with the girls in California

First Christmas, a New Church

What a strange Christmas; it was without snow. Everyone wore what I considered to be summer clothes. We found a small tree the day before Christmas and I made popcorn to string around the tree, a star made of foil paper, and oranges for decorations. Five days later was Elvira' fourth birthday, I made a small cake and we sang "Happy Birthday" in German, of course.

The church we attended was quite different from our church in Winnipeg. The women wore no jewelry, not even their wedding rings. Our girls were quite the attraction. Everyone thought the girls were so cute, singing songs in German in front of the congregation.

Members of the church blessed us in so many ways. Mr. and Mrs. Ewert and their grown daughter took us under their wings. We enjoyed meals in their home, and going on picnics with them.

Edmund still had difficulty finding steady work and I was embarrassed to constantly go to the church for help. Eventually they asked us to become members of the church. In order to meet that requirement, I had to stop wearing my wedding ring. I found this very unreasonable and argued that wearing a wedding ring was not a matter of salvation and that I could not comply. We left the church shortly after that, having been there a total of three years

.

At Forest Lawn with the Ewerts, Aug 1953

Christmas 1953

Parents Visit

During that time we moved two more times. Now we were in the town of Upland, adjacent to Ontario on the north. My parents came by train to visit. What a commotion that was in communication. By now the girls were in kindergarten and second grade, speaking English fluently and adopting the ways of their new country. Elvira, however, could still communicate with them in German. While I enjoyed having my parents visiting, it was quite stressful. Even so, I was sad when they left and I had no family around. In a few months Edmund was out of work for a stretch, and it gave us the opportunity to travel to Winnipeg to visit them.

The Klaassen Brothers move down

About that same time, Edmund's older brother, Albert and his wife, Agnes with four of their seven children moved down from Canada. Shortly after they arrived, Edmund's younger brother, Karl, his wife Sarah and their six children arrived. We enjoyed getting together with them for the holidays and other occasions.

One time, someone had given us a bunch of fish. We all drove to Mt Baldy to a picnic area for a cook-out. As the fire got hot enough to fry the fish, low and behold, no fish. To my chagrin, I had left them at home.

Another pleasant time with the families was getting together at Albert and Agnes' home and having *rollkuchen* and watermelon. Agnes made these large, thin pancakes and we sprinkled them with sugar, and then rolled them up. Oh, they were delicious. The children competed in who could eat the most pancakes and who could spit the watermelon seeds the farthest.

The cousins in California, 1959

Another move

Edmund was working more steadily so we bought our first home at 1132 East Seventh Street in Ontario. It was July 1957 when we moved in. My sister Mary came for a visit and was a big help. A year later, work was at a standstill and we moved to Escondido, renting out our home. There we lived in a hotel room until we found a house to rent. Work was steady and we enjoyed a good income, even purchasing a new car. The girls were growing up fast, Elvira, entered the fourth grade, now wanted to be known as "Vera" because kids made fun of her name in school. Linda was in second grade. The girls enjoyed getting their fifty cents allowance and going shopping downtown on Friday nights. They bought clothes for their Ginny Dolls.

The 50th Wedding Anniversary of my parents

In celebration of my parents' 50th wedding anniversary in April 1960, we made the 2,100 mile drive to Winnipeg. Many people attended the open house at their home. It was a wonderful event, but at the same time, I was saddened to see how frail my mother appeared.

While I was happy to be with my family, I was feeling miserable, sick to my stomach all the time. The smell of food made me nauseous. I was so sick Edmund put me on a train to go home while he drove with the girls back to California. Once home, I continued to feel sick but gradually I improved.

Elizabeth's Story

Chapter 9
The Blessing

July 1960, I finally went to the doctor and was shocked to learn that I was almost six months pregnant. We assumed after nine years since Linda had been born, that there would be no more babies for us. After all, I was forty-three years old. The growth in my belly and the movement I felt wasn't gas or a tumor. We were going to have a baby. The girls were so excited when we told them that they wouldn't even have to wait that long. The baby was coming in October.

In the meantime, work came to an end, our car was repossessed and our renters had given us notice they were moving out, so we moved back to our home in Ontario in September. We thought our baby was due in October, however, that was only a guess.

Shirley Ruth was born on November 11, 1960. She became the joy of our life in our later years. The girls were very excited about their new baby sister. I fear I may have put too many responsibilities on them, washing and hanging her diapers on the line to dry and then folding them. They didn't seem to mind the endless chore of keeping up with those diapers

Having a new child at this stage in my life proved to be even more precious as the older girls graduated from high school and moved on with their lives. There was Shirley to keep us active and on our toes. Even after she married, she and her husband Jeff stayed in the area. We were also able to enjoy their children.

Elizabeth with baby Shirley

The three sisters: Vera (12), Shirley (5 mo), and Linda (10)
Taken in 1961

Vera Klaassen DeMay

Chapter 10
Hard Times of a Different Kind

A few years after Shirley was born, I began a descent into deep depression. I sought help from anyone who would listen. I talked with our pastor over and over about whether this was a spiritual problem and was I not praying or serving enough? No one wanted to hear me out. People who I considered friends withdrew and didn't want anything to do with me. I felt totally isolated, desperate. I walked around the house crying all day, almost hysterical, day after day. My dear husband didn't know what to do.

Finally at the recommendation of our family doctor, I agreed to admit myself to the county mental hospital. Shirley had just started kindergarten, Vera was a senior, and Linda was a freshman in high school.

During my hospital stay, the girls had to take over responsibilities at home. Both girls were very busy with band activities. There seemed to be no support from our church. Our extended family in the area tried to help but they did not live close by. We sent Shirley to stay with one of Edmund's brothers but that proved to be too hard on her.

I was in the hospital seven weeks and endured electric shock treatments. While this was an extreme measure and had consequences such as memory loss, it did serve its purpose and alleviated my depression some. I spent most days sleeping. Shirley got herself ready for school making her own breakfast and getting dressed. I waved good bye, and then went back to bed where I would still be when Shirley got home from kindergarten.

Other difficulties

The difficulties just would not go away. My dear mother passed away. It was hard not being able to go to Canada for the funeral. Vera and I fought constantly. She made me so mad at times with her defiance, I actually broke a wooden spoon hitting her. This child was a source of deep contention between Edmund and me. I felt she adored her father but harbored contempt for me. I tried to make her obey me. Why wasn't she be more like Linda? Linda was so agreeable, so sweet. Edmund sticks up for Vera and they are quite close.

Edmund could no longer keep up with the younger men at work. The drywall sheets were much too large for him to work with. He took a job at a local wholesale nursery making minimum wage. Gradually we got behind in our house payments and had another car repossessed. Edmund's brother Albert told him one day that there was construction work in the state of Washington. After some heated discussions, we put our house up for sale.

PART III

Chapter 11
The Move to Washington

Our home sold the summer of 1967 and we made our way to Washington, not without some difficulties. Our car broke down in Paseo Robles and we ended up buying another before continuing our journey. When we arrived in Auburn, Washington, we found an apartment and Edmund began look for work. He didn't find it.

Vera stayed behind to continue her studies at the community college in California and lived with some friends from church. A few weeks after we arrived in Washington, she called to say she wanted to move up too. Edmund flew to California and then they drove Vera's car up. Now the three girls and Edmund and I were living together in a two bedroom apartment. But, the important thing was, we were together. Soon Edmund got work with the Boeing Company in Auburn, The girls started school, Vera at the community college, Linda at the local high school, and Shirley in elementary school. We found a local church and life started to look better. This move to Washington was certainly a good thing for us.

A few months after we moved to Washington, I was notified by my sister that our father had passed away. Edmund and I made the trip to Winnipeg for the funeral. Three weeks later, another call from Winnipeg brought the news that my brother Jake had suddenly died. We were not able to drive back for his service.

A year later, my husband purchased a lot in Kent Washington and we began to build our own home. Everyone pitched in. I was still struggling with the after-effects of my bout with depression and treatment so I was not that interested in making many of the decisions regarding the house.

We broke ground in September 1968. All of the work was done after Edmund's job and on weekends. The girls helped put wall framing up and nailed shingles on the roof. When Vera got engaged, even her fiancé Doug helped when he came to visit.

We moved into our home in April even though the house was not completely finished. Linda was graduating from high school in June and Vera's wedding was coming up in July. Both girls left home that summer of 1969. Shirley, who was eight years old, was our only child at home.

The family gathering after Doug and Vera's wedding
, July 20, 1969

In 1972, we were blessed with our first grandchild, a girl. Jeanice Margaret DeMay was born to Vera and Doug. We couldn't wait to see her and we traveled down to San Jose for Christmas that year. We got to see Linda also as she was living in San Francisco at the time. Oh how Edmund missed the girls. He constantly talked about going back to California. When Linda married Larry Horton, there was no telling where they would end up.

Shortly after that, I began another dark descent into depression. Once again, we were at a loss as to which way to turn, where to seek treatment. In an effort to make things a little easier on me, we sent Shirley to California to live with Vera and Doug thinking that might help. It didn't. I finally sought treatment in a mental hospital. Shirley who was in the ninth grade missed her horse and so her stay in California was short-lived.

After my time in the hospital, I noticed that Edmund started making financial decisions without consulting with me. Edmund decided we should sell our home so he could build another one with the profits we would make on the sale. We moved into some nearby apartments and I expected that we would soon be looking for property to build again. This did not to happen.

A man approached us from church with a grand investment plan. We would have part ownership in a mineral mine in Nevada that would make us wealthy beyond our imagination and be an inheritance for our children and grandchildren to come. I felt this was not right but Edmund would not listen to my misgivings and proceeded to give all the money we had for our next home. Needless to say, we never saw a penny of that money nor did we become wealthy.

The next big scheme that came up was the purchase of two lots at Lake Tapps with a partnership with Edmund's nephew Karl Klaassen. They had high hopes of building homes on these two lots and then sell them. After attempting to get the property to drain properly with no success, the lots sat there. Karl moved to another state and so they separated the lots and dissolved the partnership. Edmund still tried off and on to get something going with the property, but after a while, he gave up, and stopped paying the property taxes. Eventually he deeded the lot to his son-in-law and we were done with it. I was so relieved.

Our Twenty-fifty wedding anniversary with our three daughters and
first grandchild

Chapter 12
Retirement Years and the Long Good-bye

In 1978 Edmund retired from the Aerospace Union headquarters where he worked for the past 10 years. He was very antsy at home and so he started his own handyman business. We moved from the apartment to a small home nearby that we rented.

Shirley graduated from high school and then completed a two-year degree at the local community college. She began dating a young man, Jeff Lee, and their relationship blossomed. Soon we were looking forward to their marriage. With Jeff's family nearby, we had high hopes that at least one of our children would stay in the area.

We were blessed when Jeff and Shirley settled in the area. When they had their first child, Amy, I baby sat when Shirley returned to work. I had cared for other mothers' children in my home before this, but although I loved the baby stage, once they got to be around four years old, I was done with it. However, it was a different story with my own grandchildren. What a joy it was for me to watch Amy grow.

I enjoyed taking care of my home, planting flowers and canning fruit. Edmund and I would go pick fruit wherever we would find them. Raspberries and blackberries were abundant in our backyard. I found great pleasure volunteering at the Kent Senior Center. We went there once a week, set the tables for lunch and then ate. I did that for ten years. Another thing I enjoyed was going to the high school swimming pool for adult swim. I did that three times a week

I was enjoying having Edmund home, now that he had retired. We were involved in a Bible study together. Edmund began to be forgetful. At first it was small things such as not remembering where he put the check book, or not being able to find his glasses. I just took these as typical signs of aging. All my peers forgot little things from time to time. But when he thought he hadn't had his morning coffee and had actually had three cups already, I began to worry.

At Edmund's next doctor appointment, I brought up my concerns. The doctor examined Edmund by asking him a series of questions. Edmund knew the date, the year, the season. When the doctor asked him who the President was, his face lit up with a big grin and he replied, "Ronald Reagan." He got that one right. (He was a proud member of the Republican Party. I was not that interested in politics and it annoyed me when he sent money to support their political agendas.) The doctors said it was normal for his age (70).   We continued to carry on as if everything was normal when deep inside I knew something was not right with him. He began losing his way home from church or Bible study.

I had never driven a car before so I didn;t paid attention to which way we were going. I was no help at all. In fact I made things much worse by getting excited and questioning him over and over. In exasperation, he would yell at me to shut-up – a word we never used in our house.

Gradually, it was getting harder to ignore what was happening. He used poor judgment when driving, nearly causing an accident, I called Vera who lived in California, telling her what a close call we had just had.

"Hi Mom, what's up?" Vera asked.

"Oh, I just had such a frightful scare with your dad. We almost got into an accident. I just don't know what to do. He's going to get us killed."

"Well, Mom, if you are that scared to be in the car with him, you could choose not to get into the car, If Dad won't stop driving, and you don't have to go along," Vera replied.

One day as we were about to turn onto our street, someone hit us from behind. No one was injured. However, considering the age of the car, our insurance company totaled the car. I put my foot down and told Edmund we were not getting another car. To put my mind at rest, I got a note from the doctor, stating that in his professional opinion, Edmund was not fit to drive. I kept it in my dresser drawer, just in case.

I became very resourceful arranging transportation. One couple from church faithfully picked us up every Sunday. We used the Access van for grocery shopping and appointments Friends took me to the swimming pool. Somehow, we managed.

The constant watch as a caregiver began to take its toll on my health. I had headaches, my blood pressure was way too high, and I wasn't sleeping. Although I tried to be courageous and carry on, I made a nuisance of myself begging people to come take him out for a few hours. It is times like this when your church family can give support or draw away. I was embarrassed to keep asking. Occasionally he spent the day at Shirley and Jeff's house. I sent Edmund down to California to spend a week at Vera's. While that was great for the short time he was gone, as soon as he was home, the stress was back in full. I learned about an adult care program and soon Edmund was getting picked up at 8:00 a.m. and returned home at 5:00 p.m. four days a week.

One night in early January 1997, we had just gone to bed, when I heard Edmund get up. He fell in the hallway and he couldn't get up. I tried to help him, but I just couldn't do it. I covered him up with a blanket and six o'clock in the morning , I called Shirley to come help. She was busy getting the children ready for school so Jeff drove the thirty miles to our house to help. The hour it took him to arrive seemed like an eternity to me. Jeff got him up, helped him get dressed and we had breakfast. Edmund had a scheduled doctor appointment that morning so when Shirley arrived we took Ed to the doctor. After the examination, the doctors said he had pneumonia and needed to go to the hospital.

After a few days, they wanted to discharge him. Vera had come up from California so she and Shirley met with the discharge nurse and social worker. They were emphatic that Edmund could no longer live at home and they would not be taking him home. The girls visited several nursing homes (although they are called convalescent care facilities) and chose one located in De Moines on Highway 99. Arrangements were made for transporting him there. He would be sharing a room with another resident who was mostly comatose. We moved some of his things into his side of the room: his favorite recliner, a dresser, TV, his ceramic Percheron horses. We put some family pictures on the wall, making the room look similar to his room at home. I was so relieved that the girls had taken over. I could not have done this on my own.

When Edmund arrived at the facility, he came in thinking we had just arrived from Winnipeg. We got him settled in and after a while, we all left. Vera was staying with Shirley and when they got home, they received a call from the facility staff that Edmund had wandered out of the building and was spotted by the laundry staff. This was very upsetting to the girls and me. How could Edmund, who was so weak and could barely stand on his own, get down two flights of stairs, out a door that was supposed to be alarmed and not be spotted until he was at the opposite end of the building, What was so dangerous about this was that he was very close to the highway where he could have been hit by a vehicle. Also, it was January and very cold and he was in his pajamas and barefoot.

A week or so later, Edmund was in another critical situation. The nursing home staff communicated that the decision was up to us (Shirley and me) whether he would be sent to the hospital for treatment or not. I had a very hard time understanding what they were asking and deferred them to Shirley. The first problem was that the doctor who serviced the nursing home was not on Edmunds health care plan. There was no doctor there to treat him. Finally, the on-call doctor stepped in and when he talked to Shirley about treatment, his question to her was, "what do you want me to do? If we don't treat him, he will die, however, he does have Alzheimer's doesn't he?"

The implication was that they could choose not to treat him and he would die which was OK since he had Alzheimer's. Vera contacted her pastor who put the question into perspective. We should take the Alzheimer's out of the picture and then ask what would we do. The answer was obvious. We sent him to the hospital for treatment. What they found was that he had a blockage in his intestines, once cleared, he was good and returned to the facility.

Edmund seemed to be okay over the next week. I would get transportation to go visit him several times a week. It was very hard on me. Edmund would ask me over and over, was I taking him home now? He always wanted to go home. Sometimes he would show up at the nurses' station with his 2 ceramic horses under his arms and tell the staff he was going home.

Friday, March 14th, 1997, I was visiting with Edmund. Shirley, Jeff and the grandchildren had arrived too. Around 4:00 Edmund grabbed his chest in pain. The physician's assistant on duty that day examined him. After consulting with Shirley, the decision was made not to send him to the hospital but treat him for the pain and keep him as comfortable as possible.

He was not expected to make it through the night. It hurt me so to see Edmund suffering, it seemed as if the morphine had no effect to relieve his pain. After a while, I could take it no longer, I kissed him good-night and left. Jeff took me back to my house and I fixed myself a small dinner although I was not hungry.

I know there are some who do not understand my actions. How could I possibly leave when my husband was dying? God knows my heart and I ask that those who question my actions that night be gracious toward me.

My dear husband passed away at 8:00 PM that night. Shirley and Amy were at his side. Vera was on an airplane on her way. The girls took over the planning of the service. There was so much to do, but I was helpless to do anything include making any decisions. I was dealing with feelings I had toward my husband for not planning more for my future after his death. We never talked about it. We did no preplanning, nothing, and now it was upon me. I was extremely thankful for my daughter.

It was very rainy and dreary the day of March 17th. Following Edmund's burial ceremony at 9:00 AM, we had a memorial service at the church. Afterwards, the family gathered at Jeff and Shirley's home and we sang hymns and told stories about Edmund. The evening was heart-warming and filled with a lot of love.

Looking good

Still holding hands after forty years.

Chapter 13
Widowhood and Health Challenges

Those first six months after Edmund died went by so quickly. Although I was relieved that Edmund was no longer suffering, I missed him so much. Widowhood was full of challenges. In addition to the emotional difficulties, there were practical challenges as well, such as needing assistance with reconciling the checkbook, and keeping the house going. My son-in-law Jeff was a big help with household repairs. However, I missed my husband. We had been together almost fifty years. Yes, indeed, I missed him very much.

Life-threatening event

About nine months after Edmund passed away, I began experiencing weakness in my legs. I was falling a lot. It got worse. Shirley took me to my doctor and she could find nothing wrong. Weeks went by and I continued to get worse. Finally, when I could do nothing for myself, authorization was given to admit me to the hospital. By then I was incoherent. After several tests it was determined that I had lithium toxicity and potassium depletion. My psychiatrist had told me to increase my lithium pills without checking the lithium levels in my blood. I understand I almost died. After four weeks in the hospital, I was transferred to a convalescent hospital.

Unable to walk on my own, the instructions from the hospital were that someone was to assist me at all times. I was not to be left alone. During my first night there, I managed to get up unobserved and fell on my face. The next day, the nursing supervisor asked that we provide a night nurse as they didn't have the staffing available to do that. Fortunately, the insurance said they would cover the cost, so that evening I had an attendant with me in my room. Even with someone watching over me, I managed to fall again. The next morning, Shirley received a call telling her she had until the end of the day to find another placement for me or they would drop me off at the ER.

A place was found, the very place my dear husband had spent his last days just a year prior. My condition warranted closer observation so I was moved into the Alzheimer's unit which had a higher staff to patient ratio and was quieter. Vera flew up again (this was her third trip in two months) to help Shirley deal with everything.

The next day I got my hair done, did that ever feel good. Vera helped me take a bath that evening and tucked me into bed. She drove the hour back to Shirley's and was home just a half hour when they got a call from the staff at the convalescent facility. I had taken a fall, hitting my head and requiring stitches. They were sending me to a hospital in Seattle where the girls would meet me.

Upon my arrival at the ER in Seattle, I was delirious. I kept saying, that a man had attacked me. The girls refused to take me back after my head was stitched up and demanded to speak with a social worker about keeping me a day or two while they figured out what had happened.

In the morning they were at the facility asking questions. The staff seemed uncomfortable with the direction those questions were taking and tried to explain away the incident by saying that I had simply fallen out of bed. Well, when Vera had been there the previous day with me, she had observed a particular patient getting aggressive in the dining room. The patients in that unit were also allowed to wander into each other's rooms at will. She believed me when in my delirium I had said I was attacked and described the person.

The facility still seemed to be the best place for me. They moved me to different floor where I continued my recovery. During that time, the girls decided I should no longer live alone.

Move to Assisted Living

They found an assisted living facility for me to go to when I was discharged. The place was new and right next to the senior center where I loved to volunteer. It was also in the same town where I had lived, so I was near my friends and church.

Oh how I missed my home. The adjustment was so hard. I got transportation back to my house and planted flowers in my window box. It soon became evident that returning to live in my home would not be an option. A month after I moved into assisted living, my legs began weakening and I was having trouble walking. I couldn't even walk across the parking lot to the senior center. I accepted the fact that I would not be returning to my home and so the house was sold.

Gradually, I made new friends and enjoyed living there. The staff were very kind and helpful. As the years progressed they were able to give me the care I needed. I had several incidents where I required hospitalization and convalescent stay, however, I always looked forward to returning to my apartment.

A Devastating Diagnosis

One night I took a fall in my living room and could not reach the cord to bring help. I was in agony. I screamed out for help but no one heard me. When I didn't show up for breakfast the next morning, someone came looking for me. I was taken to the hospital where I was examined and x-rays revealed I had broken my hip. It was during that hospital stay that a doctor told me I had Parkinson's disease. Now I was presented with a whole new series of life challenges.

As the disease progressed, I had to accept the gradual loss of function in my legs. I moved from a cane to a walker to a wheelchair. I went from being able to dress myself and take a shower to needing assistance with all my basic needs. I knew if someone would just help me exercise, I could regain some use of my legs. No one was able to do that on a regular basis. Oh it could be done – for a cost.

The next challenge I was faced with was the loss of my friends. Gradually, the visits became less frequent, some due to their own deaths, others no longer wanted to drive down the hill to take me to the swimming pool, or just lost interest. Even the pastor at our church could not make a visit to my apartment when he conducted the church service at the facility once a month, I'm not judging him but I certainly thought it odd.

I must say that not everyone pulled away. There was one couple who faithfully picked me up for church on Sundays. Oh how I appreciated them. Another young couple from church made a point of visiting regularly. When they started, they just had their first baby. What joy that baby was to me. Sometimes they took me to lunch and out for a drive. They were definitely a blessing to me.

Jeff and Shirley were also very good about driving the thirty miles one-way to pick me up and bring me to their home. Sometimes I spent the night. It was always such a joy to see the grandchildren.

In June 2008, the staff notified Shirley that they could no longer provide the care that I needed. Shirley found a wonderful group home owned and operated by a Ukrainian couple. They had converted most of their home in Tacoma to accommodate five guests while the family with five kids lived in two small rooms. The home had a lovely backyard and covered patio. I spent hours out there shooting small balls into a basketball hoop. Vince and Nadia took great care of me.

My stay at the group home was not that long. In September I had a few episodes where I ended up in the emergency room. Then on September 24, I lay down for a nap and two days later, I woke up on the other side – Heaven.

Elizabeth in her kitchen

A birthday

At Bethany Care Home
July to September 2008

Shooting hoops

My last visit with my mother.

Chapter 14
Memories of Mother

I (Vera) will conclude with sharing some stories and memories about Mother... She could be very funny at times while not even knowing it.

The Hair Cut – Vera DeMay

When Mother was moved to the group home where she spent the last three months of her life, my best friend, Ann Keller, and I went up to see her. It was Labor Day weekend. Ann was a great help in communicating with mother. The first thing I noticed was Mother needed a haircut. She got her hair done once a week at the assisted living facility.

We got the owners of the care home to load mother up in the car and we drove around Tacoma until we found a small salon. I went in and asked if there was someone willing to come out to the car, drape my mothe, and cut her hair. As the person proceeded to cut mother's hair, Ann kept telling her to cut it shorter until mother's hair was shorter than she had ever had it.

Mother just sat there never saying a word. I know she wasn't very happy about her hair.

The Cat – Linda

One visit to my home in Oklahoma, Mom and I sat down to have lunch. Mom never ate without praying first. So, very seriously, she began to pray in the Old King James language. While she was praying, one of my cats jumped up on the table and started eating her food. We must have had tuna fish.

The Eye Glasses- Shirley Lee

Mother kept complaining she couldn't see out of her glasses. When my sister came up for a visit, I had her take Mother to the eye clinic where she had gotten her glasses previously. Upon examination of the glasses, it was discovered that they were not hers. When they returned to Stafford Suites and told the receptionist the story, she pulled a pair of glasses out of the drawer and asked if these were hers. Well, they were. Apparently Mother had laid them down in the beauty salon when she got her hair done one week and picked up the wrong pair.

The Ferry Ride – Vera

No one knew that Mother did not like to get out on a boat. On a family vacation with the four of us, Jeff and Shirley, and her sister Margaret made the trip around the Olympic Peninsula. On our return, the quickest and shortest way back was to take the ferry across the Puget Sound to Seattle. Well, Mother refused to get out of the van while the rest of us went upstairs to the lounge and enjoyed the crossing and something to drink. When we docked, we made our way down to the van where mother was. She was very surprised and asked "Have we left yet?"

Years later she allowed Jeff to lift her into his boat for a ride on Lake Washington. Her most excellent adventure.

Son-in-law, Jeff Lee, taking Elizabeth out for a boat ride

A Memory *from Rose Suemoto*

Elizabeth became known at family gatherings for always bringing her lime green jello with cottage cheese salad.

The following stories were submitted by Doug DeMay.

I am Elizabeth's son-in-law. We had a strange and loving relationship. I loved to tease her and she thought I was strange.

The Good-bye

Upon our leaving my mother-in-law's home after a visit, she came out to the car to say good-bye. Her words were "It was good to have you come" and then she looked directly at me and said, "it's good to see some of you go."

The Backseat Driver

We were all headed to Ocean Shores, I was driving the van with Elizabeth and her sister Margaret riding with me. Before we got down the lane where they lived and on to the street, Elizabeth starts telling me how to drive. Keep in mind that she had never driven a car in her life. This kept on until we were getting on to the freeway when she yelled "Watch out." I jumped startled and looked around for what I was about to hit. Way back in the right hand lane that I was merging on to, was an approaching car. There was no eminent danger, I had plenty of room to get on the freeway. I told her that if she wanted to drive I would pull over or she could get out of the car and find her own way back home. For the next two hours, she was silent. When we stopped to get a drink, I asked her if she would like something, she refused to answer. So I asked her sister who was laughing hysterically if she would ask her what she would like. She responded to Margaret and Margaret told me what she wanted.

I'm Japanese

On a visit to San Jose, we took my in-laws to the beach. It was a nice warm day so I took my shirt off and lay down on the blanket, enjoying the warmth on my skin. All of a sudden my mother-in-law bursts out, "You don't have any hair on your chest," to which I quickly replied, "That's because I'm part Japanese and Japanese people don't get hair on their chests." Elizabeth got a very funny look on her face and said "Really?" and my reply was, Would you have let me marry your daughter if you had known I was part Japanese?" Elizabeth looked at me and said, "Well, I don't know." I wonder if she believed me. I never told her differently.

Epilogue
Finally Home

No book written about my mother, Elizabeth, would be complete without mentioning her faith in God that carried her through the peaks and valleys of her life. She loved singing hymns especially those that talked about Heaven. You see, Heaven was her final destination, as the song says "this world is not my home, I'm just a passing through." While she was a citizen of three countries here on earth, her ultimate citizenship was in Heaven. She proclaimed Jesus as Savior, the author and finisher of her faith, to anyone who would listen.

To that end was her hope, her peace, her assurance, that this world is not the end of all things. When her time came, she simply lay down for a nap and never woke up. Two days later, her spirit departed. She is now more alive than ever before. All Praise and Honor be to God our Father, creator of all things, giver of eternal life through Jesus Christ our Lord.

Appendix
The Lichtenau Station

The train is ready for departure;
People are coming from near and far,
Walking, with spring-and ladder wagons.
Even the infant is carried there;
The air filled with dust...heaven grey;
At the Lichtenau station.

The wind blows and whistles and sings,
The child in the arms of his mother cries.
People are putting up the "Samowar"
Because one has to eat...that is for sure
Because all of them have this feeling of faintness
At the Lichtenau station.

The crowd is moving back and forth
And the hearts are heavy.
Here they are singing a song of farewell,
They know that they will never see each other again.
The man looks soberly...the woman weeps
At the Lichtenau station

Then people hurry over to the church,
They are only staying there for a brief time,
They pray and weep
And all are united in prayer.
For everyone thinks: "only trust in God!"

Whether in Canada...or Lichtenau.

The iron horse whistles and people are cold,
They lose their composure...
There is sighing and weeping – hands are shaken;
Farewell...farewell in the foreign land!"
Once more they look upon their homeland
At the Lichtenau station.

The bell rings for the last time...
One pulls up the ladder, the narrow one;
Closes the doors:
"Hand me little Lori one more time!"
And even men, grey-haired ones...
Are weeping today in Lichtenau.

The bell rings for the last time;
A sudden jerking...the train is moving!
The crowd sings:
Many persons are staying behind...alone
One waves...sees nothing because of falling tears!
Forsaken lies the village of Lichtenau.
Author Mrs. Anna Rempel

God be with you

*1. God be with you till we meet again; by his counsels guide, up-hold you, with his sheep securely fold you; god be with you till we meet again. ***
*2. God be with you till we meet again; 'neath his wings protecting, hide you, daily manna still pro-vide you; god be with you till we meet again.***
**refrain*
Till we meet, till we meet, god be with you til we meet again

Footnotes

[i] By Chr H. Homann

[ii] Mary Kornelsen, "Getragen auf Adlerflugeln" translated from German to English, Part II pages 41-43

[iii] John B. Toews, "Lost Fatherland, The Story of the Mennonite Emigration from Soviet Russia, 1921-1927.

[iv] Mary Kornelsen, "Getragen auf Adlerflugeln" translated from German to English, Part II pages 54-63

[v] Mary Kornelsen, "Getragen auf Adlerflugeln" translated from German to English, Part II pages 67-71

[vi] . Translated "Mommy, Mommy"

[vii] Translated "Come Lord Jesus, be our guest..."

[viii] Canadian Mennonite Board of Colonization, side one lists my parents and the names of their children, birthdate, and place of birth.

[ix] Canadian Mennonite Board of Colonization, side two shows the name of their town, their departure point, date of departure, date they arrived and boarded their first ship, date of arrival and departure from Southampton, England, their arrival in Quebec Canada, and the name of their sponsor.

[x] Author Mrs. Anna Rempel.

[xi] John B. Toews, "Lost Fatherland, The Story of the Mennonite Emigration from Soviet Russia, 1921-1927.

[xii] John B. Toews, "Lost Fatherland, The Story of the Mennonite Emigration from Soviet Russia, 1921-1927.

Coming Fall 2014

RETURN TO WINNIPEG

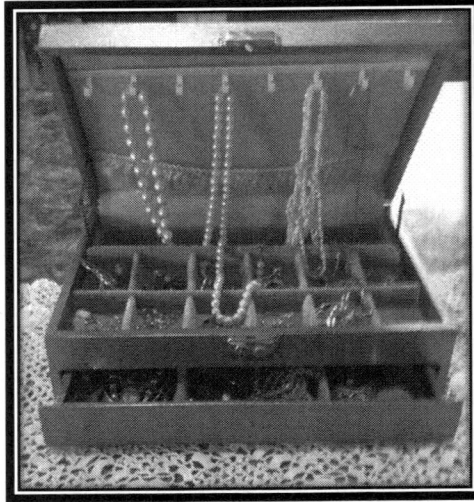

By

Vera Klaassen DeMay

A jewelry box, a few pictures, doilies, and some stained dresser scarfs is all that remains of a family. The Toews family who you met in "Elizabeth's Story." There were seven in all. The last one, Mary passed away in 2012. I ask, "What do I do with what is left? How do I preserve their memory? Does anyone care?" I could not part with these items and they sit as a shrine on my dresser reminding me of my return to Winnipeg. My head is full and I must write before the memories inside fade away.

nslated, tree

Made in the USA
Lexington, KY
29 April 2018